ALPHABET
OF
BLACK
CULTURES

JEFFREY DANIELS

For Mom and Dad

African heritage connects people in many different lands. This collection is a friendly introduction to some of these diverse and evolving cultures.

Concepts presented may not be unique to one nation nor ubiquitous in one place. Pronunciations may also vary widely from location to location.

A more detailed notes section located at the back of the book expands on each word as a starting point for further exploration.

Awale

Awale is a strategy game
played with stones in Ghana.

Balafon

Balafon is a musical instrument played in Mali.

Chukudu

Chukudu is a wooden scooter invented in Congo.

Duku

Duku is a head wrap worn
by women in Malawi.

Evala

Evala is a traditional sport
of wrestling in Togo.

Fufu

Fufu is a food commonly eaten by hand in Nigeria.

Galimoto

Galimoto is a push toy made by children in Mozambique.

Hainteny

Hainteny is poetry for sharing
wisdom in Madagascar.

Idzila

Idzila are decorative metal bands worn in South Africa.

Jebena

Jebena is a handmade pot
for serving coffee in Ethiopia.

Kanga

Kanga is a fabric useful for carrying babies in Zambia.

Litema

Litema is a patterned art painted on buildings in Lesotho.

Mento

Mento is a rhythmic folk music performed in Jamaica.

N'ko

N'ko is the written alphabet
created in Guinea.

Otjize

Otjize is a paste for decorating skin and hair in Namibia.

Plena

Plena is a dance and music style created in Puerto Rico.

Queixada

Queixada is a kick technique
for self-defense invented in Brazil.

Rap

Rap is a vocal music style popular in the United States.

Swahili

Swahili is the common language spoken by many in Tanzania.

Teleuk

Teleuk is a dome-shaped home
made of clay in Cameroon.

Ubuhlalu

Ubuhlalu are beaded
decorations worn in Zimbabwe.

Vigango

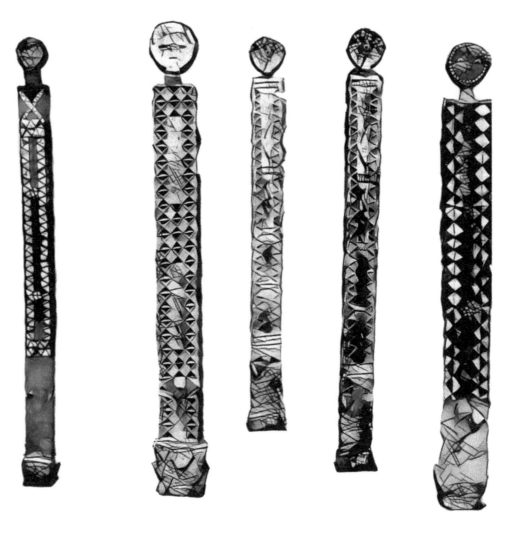

Vigango are carved wooden memorials found in Kenya.

Walimu

Walimu is the name for teachers
in the schools of Uganda.

Xiddigis

Xiddigis is the study
of star positions in Somalia.

Yassa

Yassa is a spicy meal
enjoyed in Senegal.

Zuria

Zuria is a hooded dress
worn by women in Eritrea.

NOTES

AWALE and similar variations such as Ayo, Oware, Mancala, and Warri are strategy board games. Two players compete by placing small stones into designated pits to represent planting of seeds. Each player attempts to sow (or collect) more stones than an opponent. Awale is one of the oldest known games still widely played today.

BALAFON is a musical instrument similar to a xylophone. It is made of wood and hollowed gourds, and played with mallets. While associated with Mali, it is also popular in Ghana, Burkina Faso, and Ivory Coast. In some cultures the balafon is considered a sacred instrument and used only in ritual events such as a marriage celebration or tribal festival.

Zulu ceremonial shield

CHUKUDU is a two-wheeled vehicle useful for hauling cargo. It is handmade by a specialized craftsperson with hard wood from eucalyptus trees. The driver propels a chukudu with one leg like a kick scooter. Invented during difficult economic times, chukudus are now celebrated as a testament to the resourcefulness of the Congolese people.

DUKU is one of many ornamental headscarves such as Gele (in Nigeria), Dhuku (in Zimbabwe), Doek (in Namibia), and Tukwi (in Botswana). They are colorful fashion accessories made of material that is firmer than regular cloth. Large and elaborate dukus are often worn for formal social occasions in Malawi.

EVALA is a traditional form of wrestling and a major spectator sport in Togo. Using strength and balance, each competitor attempts to push the opponent down from a standing position or out of a circular ring. Drawing international spectators, the greatest athletes are renowned for their cleverness and tenacity beyond brawn.

FUFU is eaten routinely in many West African countries. It is made by mashing yams or plantains with flour and water to create a thick porridge. Fufu is usually picked up with one's fingers and dipped in a sauce or soup. Rich in potassium but low in cholesterol, it is a healthy and popular staple food.

GALIMOTO is a push toy hand-crafted with found and recycled objects like cans, scrap wood, and old wires. Modeled after cars, trucks or bicycles, each toy is a unique demonstration of the maker's creativity and skill. Galimotos have moving parts and are pushed by hand with a long stick.

HAINTENY is a traditional form of spoken poetry shared in Madagascar. The poems are often concise and full of metaphors to communicate cultural values, philosophical views, or valuable life lessons. Hainteny are spoken at special occasions such as births, weddings, and ceremonial public speeches.

IDZILA are brass or copper bands once popular among married women in parts of South Africa. They are worn snug on the neck, wrists, or ankles as a type of jewelry. In the past these personal adornments were associated with wealth and status. Today, they are no longer common.

JEBENA is a handmade clay pitcher used for coffee preparation in East Africa. Jebenas are characterized by a long neck and round base. The vessel has been used in traditional coffee ceremonies since ancient times.

KANGA is a strong piece of colorful, printed fabric valued for its versatility. Kangas are made of resilient cotton and may be used as a skirt, a shawl, a head-wrap, an apron, a baby carrier, a sling, a tablecloth, a towel, and more.

Asante wooden doll

LITEMA is a traditional form of Sesotho mural art painted and engraved on the exterior and interior walls of homes. The stark, geometric designs hold complex, symbolic meaning or, occasionally, reference farming patterns. It is common for an entire village to gather and apply litema to a new home for social and decorative purposes.

MENTO is a style of Jamaican folk music played with acoustic instruments like guitar, banjo, hand drums, maracas, harmonica, and rhumba box. Sometimes these instruments are handmade. Mento song lyrics often use humor to comment on serious social issues.

N'KO is an alphabet invented by Guinean educator Solomana Kante in 1949. The writing system provided a standard script for the unique characteristics of several distinct West African languages. The introduction of N'ko inspired a movement promoting literacy and unity among nations. April 14 is celebrated as N'ko Alphabet Day.

OTJIZE is a perfumed paste worn by the Himba people of Namibia as protection from the desert sun. It is made from a mixture of milk, wood ash, and ochre clay giving it a deep orange-red appearance. Otjize is directly applied to the skin and hair for cosmetic and hygienic purposes.

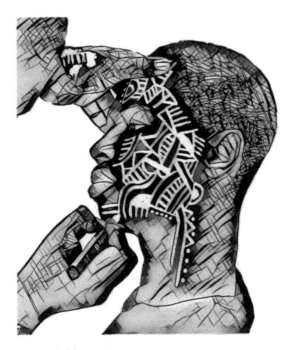

Masai tribal face painting

PLENA is a vibrant dance and folkloric music style created in Puerto Rico around 1900. Sometimes called periódico cantado (sung newspaper), the song lyrics spread messages on current events among the working class people.

QUEIXADA is a kick technique in the Capoeira martial arts, an acrobatic self-defense practice developed by the African population in Brazil. The queixada maneuver relies on balance and control to create safe distance between the practitioner and an aggressor.

RAP is a vocal music form that incorporates rhymes, vocal cadence, rhythmic instrumentals, and distinctive vernaculars. Rapping emphasizes creative use of language and rhetorical styles and strategies. It is central to the larger Hip Hop culture now found in many parts of the world.

SWAHILI (also known by its native name Kiswahili) is a linking language that connects many groups of people with different native languages or dialects. As the most spoken language in Africa, it has served as a bridge for trade and cooperation for centuries. Many Africans understand Swahili as a second language.

Resemblance of Nefertiti with cap crown

TELEUK is a dome-shaped dwelling constructed by the Mousgoum people of Chad and northern Cameroon. The structures are made of pure earth and created to blend harmoniously with the surroundings. The practical but elegant design is considered an iconic example of traditional African architecture.

UBUHLALU are beadworks used for bracelets, necklaces, headbands, and other forms of personal adornment. Color combinations carry meaning. The beads are made with a variety of materials such as glass, natural pearls, or gemstones then arranged by hand into elaborate patterns as textile art.

VIGANGO are carved wooden statues created by the Mijikenda people of Kenya to memorialize the dead. Each kigango (singular) is a unique, abstract representation of the individual honored. Veneration of the dead includes protecting and speaking to these statues. The life-sized landmarks are placed upright in the earth and considered sacred.

WALIMU is the Swahili title for teachers. Each mwalimu (singular) is tasked with imparting the accumulated wisdom and knowledge to the next generation. Like many nations, Uganda provides free primary schooling to all children in the country. Walimu are well respected for playing a critical role in the development of the community.

XIDDIGIS is the study of stars, planets, and almost any other event beyond the Earth's atmosphere. Useful for navigation and timekeeping, the study of star positions is one of the oldest natural sciences in recorded history. Mathematical astronomy existed in Africa since ancient times using the naked eye long before the invention of the telescope.

YASSA is a spicy stew prepared with onions, lemon, chili pepper, olive oil, and either chicken or fish. It is usually served with rice and can be made quickly. Yassa is one of the best known dishes in African cuisine.

ZURIA is a full-length gown with elaborate embroidery and a gauze hood. They are often accessorized with a cape called a ka'ba. Zurias are worn by women on formal occasions such as wedding celebrations.

ISBN 978-0-9760508-2-7   Library of Congress Control Number: 2020939930
www.sleepingelephant.com/abc   First edition 2020   †